# An Introduction to the Way of the Buddha

## BUDDHISM FOR BEGINNERS

By

Shalu Sharma

**Table of Contents:**

## Other books by Shalu Sharma

amazon.com/author/shalusharma

Hinduism for Beginners
Hinduism For Kids: Beliefs And Practices
Hinduism Made Easy: Hindu Religion, Philosophy and
Concepts
Religions of the World for Kids
Buddhism Made Easy: Buddhism for Beginners and
Busy People
Buddhist Teachings, Beliefs, Finding Enlightenment
and Practicing Buddhism: Buddhism For Beginners
Mother Teresa of Calcutta: Finding God Helping
Others: Life of Mother Teresa

Buddhism is a non-theistic religion based on the teachings of Siddharta Gautama, also known as the "enlightened one". It focuses not on worshipping a higher being, but on spiritual development leading to enlightenment about the true nature of life. Buddhism was founded around 2500 years ago, and today it is the most dominant religion in the East and one of the largest and oldest religions in the world.

## History of Buddhism and the Buddha

Siddharta Gautama, or Gautama Buddha, was born into a royal family of the Shakya clan who lived in the village of Lumbini in Nepal. In his royal abode, the young prince lived a life of prestige, comfort, and luxury. Until one day, he decided to leave his home and explore the world beyond. For the first time in his life, he saw an old man, a sick man, and a corpse; the experience changed his life forever. It was there that he had his first important realization: that age, sickness, and death were the in Shakya evitable fate of man.

He also saw a monk, which he took as a sign to live his life as a holy man instead of returning to his life of luxury. Thus he became a monk and studied with other holy men in search for the way to free oneself from age, sickness, and death. However, he did not find the answer in this community, and so he abandoned this life and proceeded with his quest.

Continuing his travels, which allowed him to witness the many cruelties of the world, he encountered an Indian ascetic. He was then encouraged to live a life of ascetism, and for six years, he lived a life of severe self-denial. Yet, no answer was still found, and he still was not satisfied.

Finally, contemplating about his experiences, he decided to pursue the Middle Way - a life free of poverty and suffering but also free of self-indulgence. It is said that one day, sitting beneath the Bodhi tree (at a place called Bodh Gaya, India), Siddharta meditated deeply upon the true nature of life and attained Enlightenment. With that, he became the Buddha.

Buddha started to teach people, and as his followers continued to grow, Buddhism started to flourish as a religion in India. It gradually spread to the neighboring countries, to Central Asia, East Asia, Southeast Asia, and even to the West.

## The Buddhist Philosophy

The teachings of the Buddha are centered on the attainment of enlightenment, eternal happiness, and peace, a state that practitioners call "nirvana", as well as the liberation from suffering and difficulties. It is said that Buddha did not intended for anyone to simply accept his insights but rather, to confirm these insights by themselves. The emphasis has always been on the individual's happiness and spiritual growth.

Buddha taught eighty-four thousand teachings in total. However, there are three main bodies of teachings which can be considered as the cornerstones of Buddhist philosophy: the four noble truths, the three universal truths, and the eight-fold path.

## A.    The Four Noble Truths

Buddha is often likened to a physician, and the four noble truths provide a good basis for this analogy. In the first truth, he observes the symptoms of the sickness—human suffering—and in the second truth, he diagnoses its root cause. In the third truth, he gives a prognosis—that the sickness can be treated. Finally, in the fourth truth, he prescribes the treatment.

### a.    Dukkha: The Truth of Suffering

The first truth explains that life is dukkha, or life, in itself, is suffering. Oftentimes, suffering is associated only with age, sickness, death, and bereavement, but in reality, it exists beyond these. It, in fact, lies in the very nature of life. Life is not ideal. Most of the times, life could not keep up with man's expectations, leading to a conflict between the flawed quality of life and the inherent nature of man. Even at its best, it leaves humans wanting more and more, and thus it is never truly and permanently fulfilling. This is the truth of suffering.

### b.    Samudaya: The Truth of the Origin of Suffering

Hunger, disease, loss of a loved one - these are considered immediate causes of suffering. However, the question is what causes these causes? What is the root cause of suffering? Buddha chose to go deeper than these superficial causes and discover the ultimate root of all suffering in man. This root cause is revealed in the second truth as tanha, or desire.

According to Buddha, tanha comes in three forms described as the three roots of evil: (1) greed and desire, (2) ignorance and delusion, and (3) hatred and violent urges. A visual representation of the three roots of evil exists, wherein a rooster, a pig, and a snake are illustrated. The rooster represents greed, the pig represents ignorance, and the snake represents hate. All three are connected to each other in the drawing, as a symbolism for how they reinforce each other.

### c.    Nirodha: The Truth of the Cessation of Suffering

The third truth says that one can put an end to his suffering by releasing himself from desires and negative attachment. In fact, nirvana could also mean "extinguishing", and put into context, extinguishing the three fires of greed, ignorance, and hate.

It is believed that once nirvana is achieved, the person is completely freed from the cycle of rebirth. He will reach a state of mind where there is nothing but immense spiritual contentment. This is the third truth, the possibility of liberating oneself from suffering.

### d.    Magga: The Truth of the Path to the Cessation of Suffering

The fourth noble truth details a set of principles that should be followed in order to end suffering and achieve spiritual liberation. This is the Eight-fold Path, which is also called the Middle Way as it avoids both ascetism and hedonism.

## B.     The Eight-fold Path

The eight-fold path consists of eight divisions, and each division may be done simultaneously with another as they are meant to supplement each other. The divisions need not be followed in strict order as they are listed.

### a.     Right understanding (Samma ditthi)

Right understanding refers to comprehending and internalizing Buddha's teachings, particularly the four noble truths. It is not merely about gaining intellectual understanding of the teachings, but the implementation of integration of the Buddhist philosophy into one's own perception of life.

However, the Buddha does not want people to blindly adapt his insights into their way of life. Instead, he wants them to verify these insights by applying them and deciding whether or not they proclaim the truth.

### b.     Right intention (Samma sankappa)

Right intention is the commitment to maintaining a right frame of mind, one that is selfless, unsuspecting, generous, and detached from desires. It is the cultivation of right attitudes, which must ultimately sum up to a pure and peaceful attitude necessary for enlightenment.

### c.    Right speech (Samma vaca)

Abstaining from disrespectful, malicious, or abusive language, foul words, lies, slanderous statements, and gossip - this is the meaning of right speech. Buddhist philosophy states that it is a must to speak gently and truthfully at all times. If one has nothing good to say, it would be better for him to not speak at all. One's speech must encourage harmony, not chaos and incongruity.

### d.    Right action (Samma kammanta)

Right action is living and behaving peacefully, without overstepping one's limits, burdening others, or violating the law. It refers to refraining from dishonest practices, vices, sexual indulgence, and violent behavior such as killing, torturing, or inflicting physical harm upon others. Every action must be geared towards the attainment of inner peace.

### e.    Right livelihood (Samma ajiva)

Right livelihood involves abstaining from professions that involve causing harm to others or tolerating misconduct, such as weaponry, human exploitation, animal slaughter, and selling of liquor. Furthermore, one must overcome his ego and develop his talents for a livelihood that provides common necessities for his fellow people.

**f.      Right effort (Samma vayama)**

Right effort involves strong mental discipline. It refers to cultivating a wholesome state of mind - one that is clear, harmonious, and has good will and that which does not allow any evil or unnecessary thoughts to exist. One must keep his thoughts pure, just as he keeps his words and actions pure at all times.

**g.      Right mindfulness (Samma sati)**

Right mindfulness is developing a thorough awareness of the self. This includes sensations, feelings, emotions, mental states, and the physical body as well as the internal processes it undergoes. Being alert of these things allows one to understand more of himself, and therefore be able to better lead himself to a state of peace.

One Buddhist practice that promotes mindfulness is vipassana, a kind of meditation which involves exercises such as monitoring one's own breathing as well as physical sensations.

**h.      Right concentration (Samma samadhi)**

Right concentration involves attaining the right mental focus and willpower needed to achieve all the aforementioned and, subsequently, nirvana. It involves deep meditation, wherein desires are first stripped off the mind, followed by thoughts, and finally even feelings, until what remains is a mind of perfect calm, clarity, and focus.

## C.    The Three Universal Truths

The Three Universal Truths are characteristics which are true for all living and non-living entities in the world. The three truths are impermanence, non-self, and suffering.

### a.    Impermanence (Anitya)

Impermanence refers to the dynamic and ever-evolving nature of life. Nothing is permanent in this world except for change. Processes such as formation, development, and decay continue at all times; there is simply no pause or rewind in life. In nature, this can be exemplified by rivers which flow relentlessly and plants which grow as each day passes. Time, in itself, is one of the greatest examples of impermanence. Unstoppable phenomena aren't the only manifestations of impermanence in this world, for there is also impermanence in relativity as shown by the lack of an "absolute" good or evil.

Understanding the truth of impermanence is important as it allows one to attain a more positive outlook of life. If he believes that certain things are permanent, then he would greatly grieve his losses. On the other hand, were he acquainted with the truth of impermanence, he would be able to accept his fate and focus his energy instead on newer opportunities in his life.

### b.　Non-Self (Anatma)

The truth of non-self explains that nothing in this world—be it living or non-living—possesses a permanent entity, or a "self". In conjunction with the first truth, it says that all that is impermanent is non-self.

The concept of non-self is one of the things that sets Buddhism apart from other religions. The second truth rejects the idea of "self", or the "I", which is viewed as sovereign, self-sufficient, and impervious to change. Such an entity, according to Buddha, cannot exist, as it contradicts the first truth.

The body and the mind may be attributed to the "self", but they actually do not fit its description. The body cannot be controlled by the self, while the mind can behave erratically at times and contradict the "self". Both are dynamic and impermanent.

Buddhist philosophy lays down two reasons on why it is necessary to reject the idea of a self:

(1)　It leads to more harmonious relationships.

By rejecting the idea of a "self", one would be able to prioritize others before himself. One would have no personal desires, or self-centered thoughts which can intervene in the growth of a relationship. By keeping selfish thoughts away and looking at oneself similarly as one would look at others, healthier bonds can be developed. Ultimately, it is the key to living a life of selflessness, generosity, and harmony.

(2)    It is an important prerequisite to enlightenment.

The greatest ignorance is believing the concept of a self. With this notion, there is a tendency for people to feel entitled and independent, which may lead to feelings of pride, greed, prejudice, and many more. The way to follow the path of the Buddha is to detach oneself from the concept of the sovereign "self", and focus instead on penetrating the truth of life.

### c.    Suffering (Dukkha)

The third truth states that all that is impermanent is an occasion for suffering. The dynamic nature of life can lead to suffering when people keep holding onto things. It must be understood that everything is impermanent and ever-changing, which is why emotional attachment is of little benefit to anyone. Allowing personal desires to creep into the mind will lead one to cling onto impermanent things, which will only bring him suffering once they change.

Like the two other truths, the truth of suffering is important to build up one's faith in Buddha and view life in a new light.

# Three Main Divisions of Buddhism

As Buddhism spread over the past few centuries, three main divisions of the religion emerged. One was spread in the Southeast, and the other in the Northeast, while the third is an off-shoot of the latter.

These three main divisions all started from India, the home country of Buddhism, but were developed as they were spread across different countries.

## A.    Theraveda Buddhism

Theraveda Buddhism, the Southeastern division, is the conservative branch of Buddhism. It adheres to most, if not all, of Buddha's original teachings, and relies on the oldest surviving collection of sayings of the Buddha known as the Pali canon. In this school of thought, Buddha is seen as a mere man. There is no concept of deities or higher beings, and instead the focus is on individual enlightenment. It is also believed that only through sheer effort, discipline, and faith, having followed the principles of Buddha, can one achieve nirvana.

## B.    Mahayana Buddhism

Mahayana Buddhism, which spread towards the Northeastern part of Asia, introduces some modifications into Buddha's teachings. Mahayana Buddhism regards Siddharta Gautama not as a man but as the manifestation of the divine essence of the Buddha. Thus, after his passing, many other manifestations or bodhisattvas succeeded him. One particularly famous bodhisattva is Dalai Lama, who was worshipped in Tibet. Since these bodhisattvas are considered spiritual leaders, their teachings are incorporated into the Buddhist canon. Thus, the philosophy of Mahayana Buddhism may differ from the original Buddhist school of thought.

Mahayana is also more welcoming and less limited compared to Theraveda Buddhism. In this school of thought, anyone can achieve nirvana through the grace of the bodhisattvas.

## C.    Vajrayana Buddhism

Vajrayana Buddhism, also known as Esoteric Buddhism, is an off-shoot of the Mahayana Buddhism. It is said to originate from <u>Hindu and Vedic texts</u>, which were incorporated into Buddhist philosophy. Vajrayana Buddhism stemmed from Mahayana Buddhism, and as a result it still adopts some of its philosophy. However, what sets Vajrayana Buddhism apart from the two other divisions is that it is said to provide a shortcut to enlightenment. As it undermines, to some extent, Buddhism and <u>Hinduism</u>, most of its practices are considered taboo and so its people practice in secret.

# Practicing Buddhism

Buddhism practitioners may set up an altar in their homes, consisting of an image of Buddha, candles, an incense burner, flowers, and a bowl for offering of water. Meditation is one of the most important practices in Buddhism, as it is believed that through meditation, one can connect deeper into nature, and therefore lead oneself towards the attainment of nirvana. There are different types of meditative practices which are classified as concentrative, generative, receptive, and reflective.

Buddhists go to their altars every day to meditate. There are also mantras, which are considered as a form of prayer, chanted every morning and evening. It is believed that when a mantra is chanted religiously by a person, the mantra would have an immense spiritual effect on the person.

Practitioners also go to Buddhist temples regularly to pray and meditate, and in the case of Mahayana Buddhism, worship bodhisattvas. Buddhists would sit, barefoot, in front of an image of Buddha and recite mantras. They may also listen to monks chanting religious texts, often accompanied by instruments, and pray altogether.

Pilgrimage is another important part of Buddhist devotion, as it helps foster a deeper connection with the religion. As of date, there are four pilgrimage centers in Buddhism: Lumbini in Nepal, Bodh Gaya, Sarnath, and Kusinara in India. These are places that played important roles in the life of the Buddha.

Lastly, in the case that the practitioner would like to deepen his devotion further, he may apply for acceptance as a Buddhist monk. The ceremony of ordination involves the assessment of the postulant's suitability for becoming a monk, in which if the abbot is satisfied, the postulant would be admitted into the monastic community. Shaving of the head and wearing of robes of a specific color (orange for Theraveda monks, maroon for Tibetan monks) are also important parts of the completion of the ceremony.

The specific practices involved in Buddhism depends on each sect, but what matters most is internalizing and reflecting upon Buddha's teachings, most especially the universal truths and noble truths, and following the eight-fold path. In addition to that, Buddhists must also follow the five precepts, which are written as follows:

I undertake to abstain from:

1. Killing living beings

2. Taking that which is not given

3. Sexual misconduct

4. False speech (e.g. gossip)

5. Substances that confuse the mind (e.g. liquor, drugs)

The underlying principle of the five precepts is not exploiting oneself or others. One thing to note here is the use of the phrase "I undertake", which emphasizes the free will and intent of the speaker. Buddhism prioritizes conscious decisions and commitment, which is why the five precepts is not written as a command.

Today, Buddhism remains as a strong, stable, and growing religion in many counties in Asia and even in the West. It is notably strongest in China, Japan, Thailand, Myanmar, Vietnam, Sri Lanka, South Korea, Taiwan, Cambodia, and India. One characteristic that helped Buddhism flourish is that it is highly flexible and adaptable to local traditions, as evidenced by its branches. Additionally, it gives focus to man's free choice and personal development. Without a doubt, as it continues to spread to the Western side of the globe, its growing base is one thing everyone could look forward to in the following years.

***

I hope you have enjoyed reading this short introduction to Buddhism. Here are further reading materials for your journey into the Buddhist religion.

Buddhism Made Easy: Buddhism for Beginners and Busy People

BUDDHISM: Buddhist Teachings, Beliefs, Finding Enlightenment and Practicing Buddhism: Buddhism For Beginners

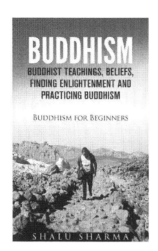

Here are some of my books on Hinduism all which are available on Amazon.

Hinduism For Kids: Beliefs And Practices

Hinduism Made Easy: Hindu Religion, Philosophy and Concepts

Hinduism for Beginners: Guide to Understanding Hinduism and the Hindu Religion, Beliefs, Customs, Rituals, Gods, Mantras and Converting to Hinduism

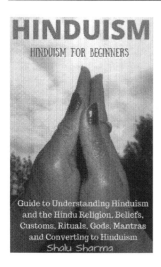

HINDUISM IN PICTURES: A Pictographic Journey into Hinduism and the Hindu Culture: Hinduism for Kids and Beginners

Thank you Shalu Sharma - http://shalusharma.com

36470468R00016

Made in the USA
San Bernardino, CA
23 July 2016